DEVOTIONS
FROM THE EARTH

Mountains

Inspired by Nature's Beauty

LINDA S CARTER

*This work is dedicated to Papa God
and the Holy Spirit that gave me endless
inspiration and insight to share these
words from an authentic and heartfelt
place. My prayer is that my efforts will
bless the Kingdom and all those who read it.*

What People are Saying:

"One thing that sets this devotional apart is its focus
on the natural world."

"I have so appreciated the author's insight into her heart and
her love of God's beautiful creation."

"Excellent writer. Linda captures the beauty of Gods
creation beautifully!"

"She impressed me in her simple childlike captivation with
the beauty of every item she sees in nature."

"A warming of my heart. This is the best way I can share what
I feel every time I open my new daily devotional."

"The book is wonderfully written and highly recommended as a
guide for morning meditations."

"This is a beautiful book."

"Easy, beautiful, lovely ... this devotional was a joy to read."

Scripture taken from the following versions:

TVT The Voice Translation
Scripture taken from The Voice™. Copyright © 2008 by Ecclesia Bible Society. Used by permission. All rights reserved.

TPT The Passion Translation
The Passion Translation®. Copyright © 2017 by Passion & Fire Ministries, Inc.

NIV New International Version
THE HOLY BIBLE, NEW INTERNATIONAL VERSION®, NIV®
Copyright © 1973, 1978, 1984, 2011 by Biblica, Inc.™ Used by permission. All rights reserved worldwide.

NLT New Living Translation
Holy Bible, New Living Translation copyright © 1996, 2004, 2007 by Tyndale House Foundation. Used by permission of Tyndale House Publishers Inc., Carol Stream, IL 60188. All rights reserved.

Contents

Week Six

The Six Week Reading Plan
This reading plan will allow you to do the short daily readings over a five day span, giving your some extra time to reflect and take a few notes on the sixth day. This routine will allow you to do daily readings Monday through Friday, have some time to journal and reflect on Saturday, and take a break on Sunday as you meet with other believers. Ask the Holy Spirit to confirm or expand on things you've read during the week in your home church.

I recommend taking some time on Saturdays to get out into nature (even if it's just your backyard) to skim over the last five readings, talk to Papa about what he wants you to learn, and jot down some notes. Make this a time of solitude to listen and learn with your favorite blend of coffee.

The journaling pages are short, so you can keep your notes brief and to the point. This makes it easy to later review what you've written, and quickly be reminded of meaningful insights. If you're someone who loves to write, you might want to do your journaling in a separate book.

Introduction

The Earth has music for those who listen.
~George Santayana

Throughout history, mountains have captivated the hearts and minds of people. I personally find pure delight in nature and things created, and mountain landscapes are the most intriguing to me.

In this devotional, we will explore the mountains by delving into their spiritual significance to uncover the lessons they teach us about our faith and our relationship with God.

My inspiration for this book came when I moved to northern California, to a small rural community and bought a cabin in the woods on the ridge of a mountain. I had always dreamed of living in a pine forest. Living in this beautiful, wild place has given me an appreciation for the things of nature that I've never had before. I was moved to write down these notes that really are a picture of my devotion to all He has given us on the Earth, and to share with others the lessons and beauty to be found.

I hope these pages will encourage and inspire you to slow down a bit and take another look at how the Earth tells us it's story, and how it all reflects the creator. He has so much to say to us through His creation!

So soak in the panoramic views and wildlife images on each page. Lean into the scriptures, personal stories and reflective questions. Glean the lessons from the mountains that guide us toward deeper intimacy with God.

~Linda Carter

Week One

Healing Mountains

Nature is our teacher, the divine force that can help
guide us towards a path of healing.
~The Wellness Station

Proverbs:16:24 TPT
Nothing is more appealing than speaking beautiful,
life-giving words. For they release sweetness to our
souls and inner healing to our spirits.

Healing experts agree that there is something about spending time in nature that is healing to our minds and bodies. Part of the reason that works is because it gets us away from stresses and pressures of life, and gives us a peaceful setting to recover. Nature brings us closer to our Creator. The things God made have a built-in design to heal themselves, and nature helps us get back in tune with that same design by which we were made.

But it's not just our minds and bodies that need healing. Sometimes our spirit being, the deepest part of what makes us who we are, is wounded. Things of the spirit can only be healed by the Spirit. I love the scripture above that teaches us how beautiful, life-giving words can release a sweetness to our souls and bring inner healing to our spirits.

Recently I went through a class that had us form small groups and do an exercise of asking the Holy Spirit for encouraging words for the people in our group, and then speaking those words over them. Then we prayed to seal those words so they would accomplish what God sent them to do. I have to say, I walked away from that class feeling lighter and inspired, with confirming words to tell me I was on the right path. It is amazing how our words, when combined with the guidance of the Holy Spirit, can heal and direct. Do you know someone who needs inner healing? Try asking the Holy Spirit for words of encouragement to speak.

Holy Spirit, I ask you for more encouraging words to share with those you put across my path. Help me to speak those words in spirit and in truth, and help those words be received to bring inner healing. Amen

Royal Cedars

The clearest way into the Universe is
through a forest wilderness. — *John Muir*

1 Kings 7:2 NIV
He built the Palace of the Forest of Lebanon a hundred
cubits long, fifty wide and thirty high, with four rows
of cedar columns supporting trimmed cedar beams.

I've always loved pine forests, and had never been in a cedar forest until earlier this year when we were looking to buy a house in a new state. I was immediately in love with the lacy leaves and stately shape of these trees. If I always wanted to live in a forest, I never imagined it could be a cedar forest! The cedars on my property are very tall, with beautiful red bark and fragrant wood. No wonder cedar wood is so coveted for building special things - even kings palaces! What a joy to live among them.

When was the last time you recognized your Father's special gifts? Sometimes We ask for things, and then forget about them. It may be years later that we are suddenly aware that God did answer our prayers! Sometimes it wasn't even a prayer, it was just a simple desire in my heart. It's those moments that take my breath away and move me to tears as I recognize the gifts of the Lord in my life. It feels like I just noticed my Father winking at me.

Answers to prayer can be so subtle that we can miss them. Take a moment today to look around and see if you can recognize anything in your life that represents an old prayer or a desire in your heart come true that you might have missed. It might be something very small, or hugely big, but when you see it, you'll know... He just winked at you!

Father, open my eyes to see the little gifts and surprises you have placed in my life. I don't want to miss a thing! Thank you for the secret things in my heart that you have always known about me, and for answers to prayers. Amen

The Mighty Oak

Think of the fierce energy concentrated in an acorn! You bury it in the ground, and it explodes into an oak!
— *George Bernard Shaw*

Isaiah 61:3 NIV
Beauty instead of ashes, the oil of joy instead of mourning, and a garment of praise instead of a spirit of despair.. They will be called oaks of righteousness, a planting of the Lord for the display of his splendor.

Y ou might be surprised at all the references to oak trees in the Bible. Some of my favorite passages talk about the "mighty oak", which seem to represent well the black oak trees on my property. Because they are growing among the tall pines and cedars, they grow extremely tall as well, competing for the sun at the top of the canopy. Many oaks that the local power company has cut down in our area are almost hollow, and I wonder how the trees ever survived like that. They are sturdy and determined trees that hang on to life even as their insides are dying. I was examining a cut out of one of our oaks and it mesmerized me for a time to study the character of the wood. The rings spoke of many good and bad years, and the cracks spoke of an extremely dry season that was upon the tree at the time of its' death. In places the bark was gone and a fibrous growth covered up the wound. These trees are resilient.

No wonder God's word speaks so often about them, using them to teach many life lessons. He compares the righteous person to a tree planted by streams of water (Psalm 1:3). I believe that when we are planted in the Lord's family, we become more resilient to the world's harshness. So when things seem hard, I need to remember and even speak out loud that the Lord calls me an "oak of righteousness", and I am a planting of the Lord to display his splendor. What a beautiful thought to distract me from a momentary spirit of despair.

Thank you Father, for calling your scriptures to my mind when I need them most. Help me to hide more of it in my heart, so I can be refreshed and redirected by your words. Amen

Grassy Fields

Flourish: Flur•ish
1. To grow well or luxuriantly, Thrive
2. To do or fare well, prosper
3. To be in a period of highest productivity, or excellence

Psalm 72:16 NLT
May there be abundant grain throughout the
land, flourishing even on the hilltops. May the fruit
trees flourish like the trees of Lebanon, and may the
people thrive like grass in a field.

Grass is one of the most resilient growing things on planet Earth. As I write this, it's the beginning of winter, and the rainy season where we live. We have been so surprised and pleased to see the grass on the hills greening up like an early Spring. It had been such a dry, hot summer - the rain is so welcome; an answer to prayer. The rain brings everything to life again.

It reminds me of how the Holy Spirit is like a refreshing rain in our lives that brings freedom and life to the dry places. When we feel dull and lifeless, we must seek the presence of the Lord.

A couple years ago I was in a spiritual dry spell. One day my husband stumbled upon a worship set online that stopped me in my tracks. I dropped everything and worshiped for forty five minutes, ending on my knees and in tears as I was drawn into the presence of God. "That's what I'm hungry for!" I said to myself. I began watching the online services from that church, a thousand miles away, and I wanted more. It sounds crazy to uproot my life and move across the country to go to a church that feeds my spirit, but it began to feel like a 'calling'. A year later we relocated to northern California to follow that call. This is home. This is where we can flourish and thrive. Come to find out we weren't the only people hearing the call. Others from all over the world were coming to this place!

Thank you Father for the dry times that make us hungry for more of you. Holy Spirit, come to us in those dry times and fill us up again. Lead us to where we need to be, to flourish and thrive in both our physical and spiritual lives. Amen

Earth Rhythms

In every walk with nature one receives
far more than he seeks. *~John Muir*

Psalm 96:11-12 TVT
Let joy be the earth's rhythm...
Let all the trees of the forest dig in and reach
high with songs of joy before the Eternal...

Most people have favorite seasons of the year. I have found that my favorite seasons can change with where I live. When I lived in the desert, the summer months were agonizingly hot, and the perfect time for a get away. Living on the east coast, I loved the colors of fall. Today, living on a mountain ridge in an oak/pine forest has given me a new wonder for all seasons, as I learn how to read the finer points in the rhythms in nature. The way the wildlife comes and goes, the dry and wet weather patterns, the grasses and moss greening up with even the slightest bit of rain. I can almost sense the joy in nature that comes with small changes and rhythms.

When I recently came across Psalm 96, I felt my heart leap! It made so much sense to me that JOY is the Earth's rhythm. I started speaking it over my trees… "Dig deep! Reach high, and praise the Lord! Let joy be your rhythm!"

Can we speak encouraging words like that over our own lives? I think we can. I think we should. Gods' Word is a powerful force when spoken with conviction and faith. I encourage you to find a scripture that touches your spirit and start speaking it over your life. Dare to believe in the promises spoken over you, even if it's you doing the speaking. Look for (and expect) the joys that come with the rhythm of Gods' Word speaking into your spirit at times that only he knows you need it.

Father, thank you for your Word - an endless source of life and encouragement. Help me to embrace the rhythms of your promises as they apply to me day by day, moment by moment. Amen

Week One Journal

Healing Mountains: How can we encourage others?

_____

_____

_____

_____

_____

Royal Cedars: Special gifts or prayers answered.

_____

_____

_____

_____

_____

Mighty Oak: Becoming an 'Oak of Righteousness'.

_____

_____

_____

_____

Grassy Fields: God's refreshing rain in a dry place.

_____

_____

_____

_____

_____

Earth Rhythms: Speaking encouraging words over your life.

_____

_____

_____

_____

_____

Other Reflections:

_____

_____

_____

_____

Week Two

Mountains Majesty

You are not in the mountains. The mountains are in you.
- *John Muir*

Psalm 48:2 TVT
Situated high above, Mount Zion is beautiful to see, the
pleasure of the entire Earth. Mount Zion, in the north...

F rom my kitchen window is a breathtaking view of Mount Shasta. I never get tired of it. I always catch my breath when I see it. When the clouds obscure it, I sigh. What an amazing gift we've been given. All the beauty of creation, and the insight and passion to be able to appreciate it.

There's a saying, "Stop and smell the roses," which reminds us to slow down and appreciate the beautiful things that are right in front of us. I spent a lot of years in a busy, stressful blur of work, raising my daughter, running a business, etc. It took so long to break out of that cycle.

Simply taking a few minutes reading daily devotions will give us the pause we need to pursue the quiet moments that bring us closer to God. But more than just a pause, we need to recalibrate. Psalm 39:6 says, "In truth, each of us journeys through life like a shadow. We busy ourselves accomplishing nothing, piling up assets we can never keep…"

Lord, help us to have wisdom in knowing what is truly important in life. Teach us to live in the sweet space of appreciating everything you've given us every day. Help us find what it is you would have us do. Life is too precious to live like a shadow. Amen

Eagles Wings

When a storm is coming, all other birds seek shelter.
The eagle alone avoids the storm by flying above it.
So, in the storms of life may your heart be like
an eagle's and soar above. *~Anonymous*

Isaiah 40:29 & 31 TVT
God strengthens the weary and gives vitality to those
worn down by age and care.... those who trust in the
Eternal One will regain their strength. They will soar
on wings as eagles. They will run; never winded, never
weary. They will walk, never tired, never faint.

The first day we arrived at our new home in the mountains, we saw an eagle soaring right over our property. It was such a blessing for us, and especially for my husband, because he has a special place in his heart for the Eagle. It was like a *sign* if you will, of God showing us we had arrived. Our journey was finally completed. That eagle sighting on that day really gave us new strength after the long hard process of buying/selling/moving and finally landing at our new place to call home.

The birds in this area are completely different than what we were used to at our old house. Instead of finches, robins and sparrows, we have eagles, hawks, vultures and turkeys. Some days you can catch the big majestic birds soaring over our property in all their glory. Everything is different here, which was exactly what God had in mind for us. It felt like we had been promoted, but little did we know, that with promotion comes more responsibility, trials and tests. We didn't know what trials were ahead, but the eagle sighting helped us know we were where we needed to be, and that God was with us.

Sometimes God speaks in unusual ways. Try opening your heart to allow him to speak to you in unconventional ways. Listen for his voice in beautiful and surprising things. He loves to give us those confirmations and little "hugs".

Father, I don't want to miss your voice in the little things. Help me to have ears to hear, and eyes to see what your Spirit is saying. Amen

Secret Places

Mountains know secrets we need to learn. That it might take time, it might be hard, but if you just hold on long enough, you will find the strength to rise up. *~Tyler Knott*

Psalm 16:11 TVT
You direct me on the path that leads to a beautiful life.
As I walk with you, the pleasures are never-ending,
and I know true joy and contentment.

Part of our property is on a steep mountain ridge, where you can easily find solitude and quiet on a short (although strenuous) walk through the forest. I cleared a small path that leads to my *secret place* and put a couple of comfortable chairs there. It's a special place that I can go to get centered in the tough times, have quiet meditation in spiritual moments, and take friends to have quiet, reflective talks.

These secret places can be very defining moments in our lives. It's where we get quiet enough to allow the Holy Spirit to lead us on the correct path of life, directing our thoughts and decisions, showing us truth from the lies, and giving us convictions to move ahead.

If you don't already have one, I encourage you to find your own secret place. A place where you can be still and listen for the Lords voice.

Thank you Father, for giving me quiet times of reflection to slow down and seek your wisdom so I can confidently walk the paths that lead to the true joy and contentment you have for each of us. Amen

Surefooted Deer

The more I see of deer, the more I admire them as mountaineers. ~ *John Muir*

Psalm 18:32-33 NLT
God arms me with strength, and he makes my way perfect. He makes me as surefooted as a deer, enabling me to stand on mountain heights.

I t's been amazing to watch the wildlife come and go in my backyard. Over time they have gotten more and more comfortable with us. I now have a critter corner setup with water and nibbles, and some of them will even come running when they hear me calling, to see what goodies I've put out for them. The deer are the most gracious and beautiful creatures coming to visit by far. After months of watching them, I am amazed at how alert they are and yet how comfortable they can be when they know there is no present danger. They can jump and run so quickly when they sense alarm, flying down the mountain and never tripping up on the forest floor or the steep terrain.

They present a beautiful lesson on being relaxed enough to let go of tensions and anxieties when we have done all we know to do, while at the same time being ready to move when the time comes for it. It takes total trust in our God (and a little patience), to do that. How often I've had to force myself to take a deep breath and let go of things I have no control over, or to wait for answers instead of forcing them. I continually have to give my worries to God and take my mind and hands off of things. I believe that the more we do that, the less we'll have to. It's okay to let go. Give your worries to the Lord. Go forward as surefooted as the deer. We can trust that our Father is working everything out for our good.

Thank you Lord for arming me with strength and making my way perfect. Help me to be so comfortable with my trust in you that I walk and run without stumbling, just like the deer. Amen

Mountain Storms

Clouds come floating into my life, no longer to carry rain or usher storm, but to add color to my sunset sky.
~ Rabridanath Tagore

Psalm 107:29-30 NLT
He calmed the storm to a whisper and stilled the waves. What a blessing was that stillness...

Storms in the mountains can be absolutely magical. Sometimes our house on the mountain ridge sets us right in the clouds, like living in the "misty mountains". The sun pokes through now and then to make rays of golden light.

The rains can be hard and steady, or gentle and soaking. The snow is quiet and fluffy. Some storms come in with great gusts of wind that shake off the dead leaves and pine needles. This can leave a mess to clean up, but when the storm passes, the trees are so fresh, clean, and sparkly. The forest seems to perk up afterwards with new growth and color.

Maybe that's the way we should look at the storms in our lives… they are a part of life that is not always bright and sun shiny, but necessary to water the deep, dry seasons and help us navigate to a clean fresh new beginning. Yes, there may be damages to clean up, but with the Lord's help we come out on the other side ready to turn the corner, and go on to whatever is next. Without the prompting of the storm, we might not move at all, and miss out on new and better things that God has for us.

Lord, help me to not fear the storms so much. Help me to remember you are there to help me through every one… ready to still the waves and lead me on to better places. Amen

Week Two Journal

Mountains Majesty: About pausing and recalibrating.

_____

_____

_____

_____

_____

Eagles Wings: How does God speak to you in unusual ways?

_____

_____

_____

_____

_____

Secret Places: Plan your next quiet time in your secret place.

_____

_____

_____

_____

_____

Surefooted Deer: Is there a worry you need to trust God with?

_____

_____

_____

_____

_____

Mountain Storms: Is a storm navigating you to a better place?

_____

_____

_____

_____

_____

Other Reflections:

_____

_____

_____

_____

_____

Week Three

The Nature of Wisdom

Look deep into nature, and then you will understand
everything better. *~Albert Einstein*

Psalm 119:98-99 NLT
Your commands make me wiser than my enemies
because they are always with me, I have more
discernment than all my teachers because I study and
meditate on Your testimonies.

If we pay attention along this journey called life, we learn lessons and become wiser and more discerning as we grow. It may take a lot of trial and error, but the lessons are there. Life is a great teacher, but I feel like I found the real treasure of wisdom and discernment in the Bible; God's Word and love letter to us. It's such an amazing and insightful book, which has spoken to me on literally every aspect of life.

So many of my "sabbatical" road trips end up in a mountain forest. It's not that the forest gives the wisdom, as much as it's the special place where I can "be still and know" my Father. It's where I can be inspired by what is created, because all of it points to him. In that state of mind, and in the special quiet places where beauty is all around, I tend to be able to listen and "hear" better.

If you're looking for answers but find that life doesn't slow down long enough to have quiet time with God, I recommend taking an overnight sabbatical trip to get away from everything so you can listen in the quiet of nature. The mountains and the forest are my favorite place for that.

Thank you, Lord, for always answering our prayers for more wisdom. Thank you for your Spirit that gives us discernment. Help us to quiet ourselves long enough to really listen and learn. Amen

A Forest Home

Forests are like churches, hallowed places. There's a stillness about them, a sort of reverence.

- Sabrina Elkins

Psalm 104:16-18 TVT
The forests are Yours, Eternal One. Stout hardwoods watered deeply, swollen with sap, like the great cedars of Lebanon you planted, where many birds nest. There are fir trees for storks, high hills for wild goats, stony cliffs for rock badgers. For each place, a resident, and for each resident, a home.

The wild places of the Earth are beautiful, and the wildlife that lives in the mountain forests are fascinating to watch when you can spy them. Cities are for people. We are only visitors in the forest, although we sometimes carve out places to call our own. God made a place for everything to live. How special it is to live among the wild things.

The does and bucks wander through my property like they own it (actually, they do!). The blue jays and smaller birds come to help themselves to seeds the turkeys leave behind. Then the squirrels and rabbits started coming to see what might be there for them. The deer like to come for the bird seed, apples and carrots. A doe and her baby look for my treats regularly. And the turkeys roost in the trees on my property sometimes. How sweet to share the forest with them.

Let's never lose our childlike wonder for the things of creation. When we see how nature works in harmony for every living thing, we can know it's not an accident. It's intelligent design by a loving, very creative God. Take a breather from man made cities and visit the forest once in a while to remember the wonder of nature. The wonder of creation.

Thank you, Father, for the beauty of nature and wildlife that shows us what an amazing God you are. Help us not to lose our childlike faith. Amen

Mountain Birds

Be as a bird perched on a frail branch that she feels
bending beneath her.. still she sings away all the same,
knowing she has wings. ~*Victor Hugo*

Psalm 50:11 NLT
I know every bird on the mountains and all
the animals of the field are mine.

Some birds and animals you can only see in the mountains. To get a glimpse of a soaring eagle or a white owl is so special and rare. The wild turkeys have been coming around by the dozens to my clearing behind the house, What fun it is to watch their antics as they go about their scratching and searching for food. They are big beautiful birds - and a real treat to see them open up their feathers in full display. I started sprinkling bird seed for them, and over time they have become almost friendly, making a cooing noise when I come out with the seeds.

All this beauty belongs to the Lord. We are only stewards as he sees fit to give us what ever small part he thinks we can handle. The scriptures tell us that when we do well with the small things, he will give us more responsibility. My pastor once taught that more responsibility *is* the reward the Lord gives. Years ago I worked my way through a very difficult workplace situation with integrity. The only way I could do it was remembering that I don't work for men, I work for the Lord. That experience led to starting my own business, and I'm sure that was the reward for doing my best, even for a demeaning, hotheaded boss. Those days were filled with so many prayers for that man, and for my own patience! In the end, God actually used that man to help me get started being my own boss! I have to laugh at how that worked out... He really does work all things together for our good.

Thank you for the challenges and tests, Lord, they always lead us from glory to glory when we follow your ways. You are a good God. All the time. Amen

Mountain Songs

Sing a new song unto the Lord; let your song be sung from
mountains high. Sing a new song unto the Lord, singing
alleluia... *(Song by Dan Schutte)*

Isaiah 42:10-12 NIV
....Sing a new song to the Eternal... The peaks of
mountains, too, raise your voices with a great,
glad cry. Let them all give glory to the Eternal.
Let them praise the One who is, was and will be
heard along the coasts.

We write songs about singing to the Lord on the mountaintops, and the Lord writes songs about the mountains themselves singing to him with great glad voices! Somehow the mountains, and in fact all of creation know their Creator. "Let all creation rejoice before the Lord..." (Psalm 96:13) Sometimes I can see rejoicing in the simple beauty of a flower blooming, giving it's all for the Lord. There was a day when people were born knowing our Creator, but that all changed many thousands of years ago in the Garden of Eden. Now, we are born into adversity and must search for him as for hidden treasure to know him. It's not automatic for us to find our Creator any more, but this is our destiny.

"All creation waits in eager expectation for the children of God to be revealed." (Romans 8:19) The "children of God"... that's us - the people who do find the hidden treasure of Jesus. What an amazing picture: all creation is watching the plan of the Lord unfold for us, his children, waiting for us to be revealed. In the waiting, all creation raises their voices to praise the God of creation. Even the angels watch in expectation; helping us along the way, and rejoicing when each one of us turn our hearts to God and welcome him in. (see Luke 5:9-10) Now we are also waiting for all to be revealed. We know the truth, and it has set us free, but there are so many others that are lost. We must help them find this treasure as well. This is also part of our destiny.

Lord, thank you for opening our eyes and hearts to know you. Show us how to work with you in guiding others to find the treasure of Jesus. Amen

Note: Stephen Curtis Chapman wrote a beautiful song called "The Treasure of Jesus" which you can find on YouTube.

Hiding Places

Right before I gave up, You saved me, You saved me. One
night you fell down from the stars, shining a light into the dark,
and you picked up all my broken parts.
(You Saved Me Song lyrics by Jake Miller)

Psalm 40:2 TVT
He reached down and drew me from the deep, dark
hole where I was stranded, mired in the muck and clay.
With a gentle hand, He pulled me out to set me down
safely on a warm rock; He held me until I was steady
enough to continue the journey again.

The mountain forests are beautiful, inspiring, and a wonderful place to seek the Lord to get centered. Sometimes on my worst days they provide a hiding place from life's pressures. Did you ever feel like you want to run away from everything? Yeah, me too. Now I know that running away doesn't solve anything, but sometimes a "get away" is just the ticket to take a breather and get with God about some serious business going on in my life. When my problems are caused by my own mistakes, they can be the hardest to overcome.

But the Lord is faithful to help me find myself, my beautiful self, again. Spending alone time with God helps me remember who I am in him. Just like the scripture above says, he pulls me out of my own mucky muck and helps me wash away all the bad feelings, forgive myself and others, and move on. Everyone has trials, and though they weigh heavy on us at times, we must face them, ask for forgiveness and let them roll off our shoulders.

In the book of Philipians, Paul says, "But one thing I do: Forgetting what is behind and straining toward what is ahead, I press on toward the goal to win the prize for which God has called me.." Living in the past and dragging our baggage with us doesn't work.

Papa God, thank you for always bringing me back from the muck and mire and setting me up on the high places, on the warm rocks, and holding me in your loving arms, listening to all my prayers, and drying all my tears, until I am ready to continue my journey again. Amen

Week Three Journal

Nature's Wisdom: Reflect on spending time with nature.

_____

_____

_____

_____

Forest Home: Write about the wonder of creation.

_____

_____

_____

_____

Mountain Birds: How to be a better steward of God's gifts.

_____

_____

_____

_____

Mountain Songs: About your destiny in finding Jesus.

_____

_____

_____

_____

_____

Hiding Places: Ask Papa God to pull you out of the muck.

_____

_____

_____

_____

_____

Other Reflections:

_____

_____

_____

_____

_____

45

Week Four

Mountain Meadows

Cross the meadow and the stream and listen as the
peaceful water brings peace upon your soul.
~Maximillian Degenerez

Psalm 118:5-6 TVT
When trouble surrounded me, I cried out to the
Eternal; He answered me and brought me to a wide,
open space. The Eternal is with me, so I will not be
afraid of anything.

The forest is pretty thick where I live, so it's nice to come across meadows when driving or walking about. Sometimes I like to pause and stay in the wide open areas for a few minutes. They somehow represent a safe place. Maybe it's because I can see more of what is in my immediate space. The sky is wide open, and I can relax.

When I found what Psalm 118 said about the "wide open spaces" being the Lord's answer to save people who are surrounded by trouble, I started speaking it when I found myself in any kind of trouble or dangerous place. When I feel backed into a corner by circumstances, or when I am out riding my motorcycle in rush hour traffic, I thank the Lord for 'wide open spaces'. There is lots of room to see clearly and get through what ever is causing me fear. It turns out that most times, the fear was the worst of the situation, and nothing bad ever happens. The Lord takes care of me and teaches me day by day to trust him more. Less fear, and more peace each time I speak out my faith in the middle of it. The next time you're afraid, try asking for your wide open spaces.

Thank you again, Lord, for your words that I can lean on when I need help. Thank you for wide open spaces to give me protection from the fearful things in life. If I had perfect faith, I might not fear at all, and you increase my faith a little more each time you turn my fear into peace. Amen

Deep Truths and Hidden Secrets

Go to the trees to explore your questions and dreams.
Go to the trees to desire and seek. The world will
listen as you walk, watch, soften and breathe.
~*Victoria Erickson*

Daniel 2:21-22 TVT
He gives wisdom to the wise and grants knowledge
to those with understanding. He reveals deep truths
and hidden secrets.

I have worked from home for thirty years, but I have never had such an inspiring view from my desk as at this house in the forest. When the deer and other wildlife wander through my property within view of the window, it can be hard to concentrate on work. Other times when I get stumped by some computer dilemma, I take a break and step outside or gaze out the window into the woods to gather my thoughts and clear my head. A quick prayer is the usual course of action, asking God to give me wisdom beyond my years to figure things out and do a good job.

Let's not forget how easy it is to glean wisdom from the Bible. In his book, The Wisdom of God, AW Tozer wrote: "We have degraded Christianity to be a kind of soft vaccine against hell and sin... The purpose of God in redeeming men was not to save them from hell only, but to save them to worship, and to allow them to be born into that eternal wisdom that was the Father." The back cover description for the book says, "Wisdom is not some highbrow philosophical concept, but rather a highly practical tool for living the best possible life." If we want to have the best possible life, we just need to find and apply God's wisdom. The hidden secret about all this is that it's so simple. Tozer taught from the scriptures of Paul that eternal wisdom was fulfilled in Jesus. Our journey to wisdom starts by deciding to follow Jesus. Is there anything hidden from you that you need wisdom to understand? Let's ask God for it...

Papa God, thank you for revealing deep truths and hidden secrets to us. Thank you for continuing to giving us wisdom for the every day details of life when we turn to you. Amen

Giant Redwoods

Count your age by friends, not years. Count your life by smiles, not tears. - *John Lennon*

Joshua 13:1 TVT
You have grown old and there is still work to do...

The giant redwood forests are magical places. The first time I saw them I was awestruck. It was like I had been transported to a real enchanted forest you read about in The Lord of the Rings. There is a road called "Avenue of the Giants'"along the California coast that drives through the middle of a large giant redwood forest for miles. There are endless trails to walk among them with unusual giant ferns and clover along the path that I've never seen anywhere else. It's a wonder how they still exist in our time. Some have even been alive since the time of Jesus. Just think about what these old trees have seen and been through. But they hold on year after year to just be in the world for all to see and admire. If that is their only job, they do it well.

Are we ever too old to make a difference in the world? I don't think so. In fact, the older we are, the wiser we are, so we are far better equipped to mentor others or set an example. Older men and women can teach the young men and women how to live godly lives (see Titus 2). Even if you're still young, there will be someone younger than you to be a hero to. That's the way of the Kingdom, and there's still work to do.

Lord, help me to be the kind of person that can be used by you to be a godly influence to those around me... no matter how old I get. Amen

Walking in Love

The journey only requires you to put one foot in front of the other... again and again and again. And if you allow yourself opportunity to be present throughout the entirety of the trek, you will witness beauty every step of the way, not just at the summit. *Unknown*

1 Corinthians 16:14 TPT
Let love and kindness be the motivation
behind all that you do.

Walking mountain trails is so pleasing and refreshing. There are serious hikers who like the challenge of a hard climb and like to press in to make it to the tops of summits, and then there are folks like me who just like to meander along the easy green trails taking in the view. Every walk in the woods is like a little adventure in the journey of life. There is always new beauty to see and inspire.

When I lived in Phoenix some years ago, I used to get together with a couple of girlfriends for walks. We used to call them our "Walk of Faith" because it always turned out to be such a great time of ministry to each other as we shared the good and bad things going on in our lives. We rejoiced about the good things, or prayed for each other's needs. Fellowship with other believers is so sweet because we have that "kindred spirit" that brings us together in a shared faith, and in the love of Christ. It's also such a joy when others can see the love between us that makes an unexpected imprint on their hearts. Sometimes that is all it takes to plant a seed in an unbeliever's life. It's like a natural ministry that happens without us even trying. We just let our love and kindness for each other be seen, and it makes a difference.

Thank you, Father, that you don't waste anything. I pray you will continue to use me in natural and even unknown ways. Let my life be a testimony to you. Amen

Mountain Refuge

I always wanted to live in a log cabin at the foot of a mountain. I would ride my horse to town and pick up provisions. Then return to the cabin, with a big open fire, a record player and peace. - *Linda McCartney*

Psalm 2:12 TVT
But blessings await all who trust in Him.
They will find God a gentle refuge.

If you've ever been to a cabin in the woods, you know what a special retreat they can be. When I was a young girl, I read a book called "My Side of the Mountain", which was about a young boy about my age (at the time) that ran away to the mountains. He lived in a hollowed out tree and made friends with the wildlife. I used to day dream of doing it too. What a great adventure that would be... or so I thought at the time. Now that I'm older and wiser, I can't imagine what a crazy scary idea that would be. I mean a cabin in the woods is one thing, but living in the wild, that is quite another. I am very thankful to have a strong, sturdy home to be safe and secure in the world.

But in this life, there is more than just our physical safety to think about. If you've been awakened spiritually in even a small way, you know there is more. Our Father has put eternity in our hearts, and I know the only true safe and secure place is trusting in him. He protects us in this life, and the one to come. He is the place our hearts and souls can take refuge.

Thank you, Lord, for giving us the sense to know you deep in our spirits, and to know that you have a plan for us. Thank you that we can know you are there for us to run to in every situation, and believe you will bring us to be with you one day. Amen

Week Four Journal

Mountains Meadow: Do you need safe, wide open spaces?

_____

_____

_____

_____

_____

Hidden Truths and Secrets: A scripture that reveals truth to you.

_____

_____

_____

_____

_____

Giant Redwoods: How can God use your talents?

_____

_____

_____

_____

_____

Walking in Love: How can your love and kindness be seen?

_____

_____

_____

_____

_____

Mountain Refuge: How can God be your refuge today?

_____

_____

_____

_____

_____

Other Reflections:

_____

_____

_____

_____

Week Five

High on a Hill

For we must consider that we shall be as a city upon a hill. The eyes of all people are upon us.
John Winthrop dreams of a city on a hill; 1630 before settlers reached New England

Psalm 62:6
He alone is my rock and deliverance, my citadel high on a hill; I will not be shaken. My salvation and my significance depend ultimately on God; the core of my strength, my shelter, is in the True God.

When I lived in Arizona, I used to visit the Grand Canyon on a regular basis. There is really nothing that can compare to the majesty of this place. There before your eyes is the most amazing landscape and evidence of Noah's flood we can find on planet earth. There are many secular arguments about how it was formed, but just from looking at it, my common sense agrees with creationists who say it must have been a cataclysmic event on a gigantic scale. First, you see all the different soils that were deposited in perfectly flat layers as the water was moving and swirling the earth in a global flood. Then to imagine the amount of water that must have been present to carve out the canyon as the water was receding. Together with volcanos and earth quakes, mountains rising and falling. What a crazy time for planet earth! But the evidence is there for all to see, so we are without excuse.

Today you can sit on the edge of the deep canyon high on a rock and gaze fifteen miles across to the other side. What a testimony of how beauty can come from ashes. That high rock gives us a vantage point that can make the whole event clear. It makes me think about the scripture above - how our Lord Jesus is our "Rock", our strength, our shelter. He sets us high on a hill with a great vantage point so we can see a bigger picture of what is going on in life, and not be shaken. Yes, there are things in life that will shake us up, initially, but that's when we gather our strength and look out from our vantage point and shake it off.

Lord I am in awe of the beauty you gave us here on planet earth, and how it all points back to you. Thank you for the strength you give us and the vantage point of seeing things from a heavenly perspective. Amen

Mountain Pass

Difficult roads often lead to beautiful destinations.
~Unknown

James 1:12 TPT
If your faith remains strong, even while surrounded by
life's difficulties, you will continue to experience the
untold blessings of God!

When I was younger, I was fearless about driving on mountain dirt roads that led to who knows where, on the edge of cliffs with no room to pass should an oncoming car come along. I really thought it was an adventure everyone would love, but I found out I was sorely wrong when I took my brother and sister-in-law (who were visiting from another state) on a 'scenic route' home from Cripple Creek, Colorado on a precarious back road. What started out as a fun outing, turned into a trip of horrors for my guests. My giggling about their fears (trying my best to make light of a bad situation) didn't help. It wasn't just a scary ordeal for them. I was suddenly someone they despised and wanted to get away from as soon as possible. They left for home sooner than planned. I felt horrible and sincerely apologized, but the damage was done.

Sometimes life can be difficult when unexpected things happen from bad decisions made. Even with no bad intentions, we still have to deal with the heartache of a wrong turn. It's easy to get depressed when things go wrong, and sometimes I allow myself to wallow in that place for far too long. Eventually the time comes for me to snap out of it, and of course I turn to my Father. My faith is what always pulls me back to the place of blessings. It's when we're in the middle of our difficulties and turn back to our faith that we rediscover the blessings that have been waiting for us all along. Is it time for you to let your faith pull you back to a place of blessing?

Lord, when I'm in a difficult place, please help me to keep coming back to you. Show me the way back, especially when I can't see it clearly. Amen

Mysteries

The "Mysterious Mountain" Symphony was written in
1955 by Hovhaness, who commented: "Mountains are
symbols, like pyramids, of man's attempt to know God."

Psalm 73:16 and 26 TVT
Trying to solve this mystery on my own exhausted me;
I couldn't bear to look at it any further. So I took my
questions to the True God... I admit how broken I am in
body and spirit, but God is my strength, and He will be
mine forever.

The view out my kitchen window shows vistas of mountains and the grand peak of Mount Shasta in the distance. The shadows in between mountain ranges always intrigue me. Is it pure wilderness out there? Is there a road somewhere to explore those hills? I may never know, but I love the mystery. It seems that God gave a curious heart to each of us that draws us to the unknown. It makes me understand a little about why mountain climbers have to climb to the top, just to say they've done it.

There are other times when life's mysteries are not so interesting or intriguing. When life's troubles are weighing me down and I'm pressed to make hard decisions, it can be unbearable. I imagine everyone goes through anxious, trying times. It's part of the human condition, and if I didn't have my Father to turn to, I honestly don't know how I'd get through some of those difficult times. When I think about the people in the world who don't know Him, it truly saddens me to think of what a struggle life is without having the strength of the Lord to lean on. I love finding nuggets like the passage in Psalm 73 that tells me there is nothing unusual about what I'm going through, because someone thousands of years ago faced a similar dilemma and shared how they found the answers. They admitted how exhausted and broken they were and turned to God for their strength. The deeper we look into the Word of God, the more we find that the answers are always in there.

Thank you Father for giving us your precious words of guidance in the Bible. Thank you for the stories that show us we are not alone, that the troubles we have are not unique to us, and that you are always there to give us strength. Amen

Gold Mines

Refine: re•fine
remove impurities or unwanted elements

Proverbs 17:3 TPT
In the same way that gold and silver are
refined by fire, the Lord purifies your
heart by the tests and trials of life.

When I lived in Arizona, I bought a cabin near a remote, hundred year old mining town called Crown King. Half the adventure of spending time at the cabin was getting there - it was twenty eight miles of rough washboard dirt road to the town, and then another eight miles of an even rougher 4x4 road full of ruts and boulders to get to my cabin. In the town's hey day the town drew in people to try to "strike it rich" in gold mining. It seems that people are still trying to find the easy path to riches. A few may get lucky, but for the most part it takes hard work, and trying and failing a few times before you are successful at starting a business or climbing the ladder in a career.

In the same way, there is no instant way to become a godly, righteous person. It's a journey that may take a lifetime. Saying yes to Jesus is only the first step. God gives us opportunities to grow and learn by way of the tests and trials we have in life. It took me some years to figure this out, but I am finally getting it when the Bible says to "consider it pure joy when we face trials" (James 1:2), because God is building our character. Sure, I get frustrated by some of life's ups and downs, but I've learned to look for the lessons. Even if I can't quite define the lesson, I am learning to find peace in trusting that my Father has good plans for me, and is working everything out for my good, in spite of what I may be going through. Are you looking for the lessons in your difficult situation today?

Thank you, Lord, for purifying my heart and making me into a better person. Help me to see the lessons I need to learn so I can develop the character I need for the rest of the journey, and beyond. Amen

Moving Mountains

Earthquakes move mountains. *-Mitigation Works*

Psalm 46:2-3 TVT
No fear, no pacing, no biting fingernails. When the
earth spins out of control, we are sure and fearless.
When mountains crumble and the waters run wild,
we are sure and fearless. Even in heavy winds and
huge waves, or as mountains shake,
we are sure and fearless.

The last couple years of living in a pandemic has felt like the world is spinning out of control for sure. It's been a crazy, wild ride with so many unexpected side effects of a tiny microscopic virus, that has left the whole world in a mess. Nothing will ever be the same. They say there's a "new normal," and all of us are trying to adjust. So much loss, so much heartache. How do we overcome this "spirit of fear" that has gripped the whole world?

The answer is to stand on our Rock, Jesus. This seems like such a simplistic statement, but most things with God are simple and profound like this. As the scripture above states, we are "sure and fearless" in the face of all the world issues when we have the Holy Spirit living inside us. We can know that no matter what is going on around us, we are secure in the Lord. Yes, there will be hardships and sickness in this life. I'm not saying we can get out of any of it. But there is a peace deep inside a believer's heart that can't be denied or explained. It is what gets us through even the chaos of a pandemic.

If fear is trying to get a grip on you, let it go right now. Give it to Jesus and stand on the Word that says we are "sure and fearless". Activate your faith; say it out loud, "I am sure and fearless", and lean into it. "God will never give you the spirit of fear, but the Holy Spirit gives you mighty power, love, and self-control." (2 Timothy 1:7 TPT)

Papa God, thank you for being my strength and my rock through the tragedies of life. Help me to keep coming back to that "sure and fearless" heart. Amen

Week Five Journal

High on a Hill: What do you need to shake off today?

_____

_____

_____

_____

_____

Mountain Pass: Coming back to God's place of blessing.

_____

_____

_____

_____

_____

Mysteries: Find the answer to a problem in God's Word.

_____

_____

_____

_____

_____

Gold Mines: *How are you growing through tests & trials?*

_____

_____

_____

_____

_____

Moving Mountains: *About letting go of a fear you have.*

_____

_____

_____

_____

_____

Other Reflections:

_____

_____

_____

_____

_____

Week Six

Restless Spirits

When I saw the mountains the weight lifted and my
restless spirit calmed... I knew I was where I belong.
~Unknown

Galations 4:6 TPT
And so that we would know for sure that we are his
true children, God released the Spirit of Sonship into
our hearts, moving us to cry out intimately, "My
Father! You're our true Father!"

It's amazing how nature can bring us back to center when our spirits are out of sorts, and our minds are stressed. All our modern advancements and technologies have brought us many comforts in life, but there is nothing that can make us feel more at home like getting back to nature. For me, it's like some kind of deep inner feeling that we are connected to Earth in ways we can't explain.

In the same way, the Holy Spirit living within us is the thing that lifts our restless spirits to know in the depths of our hearts that God is our true Father. This was a real healing experience for me, because I never really had a loving father figure in my life. I remember the day the Holy Spirit set this knowledge into my heart. I was in a Vineyard Church service, and the pastor gave a word of knowledge that the Lord wanted to heal the hearts of the fatherless. All I had to do was receive it. Well, I knew that was for me, but there were many others touched that day as well. In that instant of surrender, I knew that God was my Father; has always been my Father, and he loves me just the way I am. He adopted me to be his own. I am not alone or unwanted. That revelation broke something in me. My hardened heart was healed that day. Oh how sweet it is when the Holy Spirit leads us to places of healing. What freedom there is when we lean into it! I encourage you to lean into those moments when you feel God speaking and asking you to release something to him. Don't hold back; let it go and be healed.

Thank you Holy Spirit for leading and guiding us on the paths of healing and into a deeper knowledge of your love. Amen

The Beauty of Nature

Nature is the art of God. *~Dante*

Job 12:7-10 TVT
But ask the animals, and they will teach you, or the
birds in the sky, and they will tell you; or speak to the
earth, and it will teach you, or let the fish in the sea
inform you. Which of all these does not know that the
hand of the Lord has done this? In his hand is the life of
every creature and the breath of all mankind.

O ur God is truly an artist. One of my favorite things to do is go exploring new places in nature. I love to drive to new destinations and spend time just gazing at more of God's beautiful creation. The southwest has the most spectacular landscapes I've ever seen. The red sands and monuments, the arches, and the magnificent Grand Canyon are truly inspiring. These kind of experiences live in our hearts and memories, and become a part of us. Things and people may come and go during our journey through life, but the beauty of nature and our time spent in it makes an impression on our soul that stays.

When was the last time you took some time out to marvel at creation and let it refresh your soul? I'm not talking about a vacation with every minute packed with activities and thrills like a theme park, but a quiet time away from everything where you can really still your spirit and rest. A time to see some natural beauty and soak it in, thanking Papa God for the wonderful creation that he has given to us. This is the essence of being still and knowing God. Speak to him and wait to hear his still small voice. "Blessed are those who listen to me, watching daily at my doors, waiting at my doorway. Those who find me find life and receive favor from the Lord." (Proverbs 8:34-35 NIV) Now that's my kind of R&R.

Father God, I stand amazed by the beauty you created in nature. Thank you for giving us richly, all things to enjoy. (1 Timothy 6:17) Amen

Challenging Trails

It's only after you've stepped outside your comfort zone
that you begin to change, grow, and transform.
~ *Roy T. Bennett*

Ephesians 2: 22 TPT
*This means that God is transforming each one of you
into the Holy of Holies, his dwelling place, through the
power of the Holy Spirit living in you.*

C ompleting a challenging mountain trail can change your life. I think it has something to do with facing and overcoming our fears, that really transforms us. I have several friends who have hiked to the bottom of the Grand Canyon and back, and they really do come back inspired and confident. I cannot hike the Canyon due to a foot ailment, so I opted for rafting through it, which proved to be just as challenging and thrilling for me. I believe it's the challenges in life that cause us to grow in character and self-esteem. I have personally found that pressing into a challenge, rather than shrinking back, is where the real growth happens.

The biggest transforming experience in my life was choosing to follow Jesus. I knew I needed him, but I really had no idea about the challenges ahead of me. I didn't realize I was signing up for the Holy Spirit to change me from the inside out to make me into his dwelling place. What a high honor! I'm sure if I knew this was the point, I might have shrunk back feeling like I was wholly inadequate for the job. In fact that kind of thinking kept me from surrendering to him for some time. But my need for him finally outweighed my insecurities about being good enough, and I stepped out in faith into the greatest adventure of my life. Since then the Lord has brought me through low valleys and over high mountaintops in the process of healing the innermost parts of me, which has been the "challenging" part. But the view from here (thirty nine years later) is beautiful and amazing. Are you pressing into your spiritual adventure, or shrinking back?

Thank you Father for giving me the boldness to press in when you are leading me through the mountaintops and the valleys of life. Amen

Pine Cones

The words of God are not like the oak leaf
which dies and falls to the earth, but like the
pine tree which stays green forever.
-Mohawk Wisdom

Proverbs 27:9 NIV
Perfume and incense bring joy to the heart,
and the pleasantness of a friend springs
from their heartfelt advice.

Have you ever looked closely at a fresh pine cone? There are many styles and shapes, and a short study in my own back yard has amazed me at their diversity and beauty. The fir trees, which look like your typical Christmas tree, actually have small pine cones with paper thin petals, yet their colors and patterns match the giant pine cone petals from the sugar pine tree. Some pine cones are smooth and others are prickly! The ponderosa pine have the typical pine cones we think of in shape and size, and they are abundant around my property. They seem too beautiful to just rake up and throw away, so I started researching the many uses for them and got creative. There are a lot of ways to use pine cones.

The same could be said of how we use our words. Sometimes they are caring and bring encouragement to others, and other times our words are hurtful and prickly. It seems I'm constantly trying to figure out how to be more gracious and loving with my words. How I wish all my words were as beautiful as a fresh pine cone. I have pine cones around my house, and when I need to get control of my words, I can pick one up and turn it in my fingers to help give me pause in the conversation. I feel the prickly points and remember not to speak that way to those I love. Maybe a pine cone around your house can help you from being too prickly with your words too.

Papa God, continue to help me with my words. Continue to show me the life lessons I need to speak heartfelt advice to those who hear me, and may I more often than not, speak out of love. Amen

Mountaintop Moments

At some moments we experience complete unity within us and around us. This may happen when we stand on a mountaintop and are captivated by the view.
~Henri Nouwen

Matthew 14:23 TVT
After He had sent them away, He went up the mountain by Himself to pray. When evening came, He was there alone.

Mountaintops are physically hard places to get to. Maybe that's why they have such a special effect on us. We know that so few have been there, and it ignites something inside us that makes us feel whole when we experience that unmistakably unique moment in our life that may never come again. This must be what drives mountain climbers to conquer the mountain tops of the world.

Jesus made a habit of going to the mountain tops to get alone and pray during the peak of his ministry. It's something we can learn to do, to strengthen our ministry and our own walk with God. I'm not a big hiker, but I do love to drive to the mountains to be inspired and get some alone time with God. If it was good for Jesus, it's got to be good for me!

Another way we experience mountaintop experiences is on the inside, in our spirits. It's those moments in life that bring great rejoicing, and during those moments we feel on top of the world; your first job, your wedding day, completing a long hard project, the day you said yes to Jesus. We would love for every day to have high moments, but real life is not like that. When the road leads us to the valleys, that's when we can recall the mountaintops and know this is only temporary. We can push through and look for that next day of rejoicing. If you find yourself stuck in a valley, don't stay there. Get up, get out and go find a mountaintop! Ask the Lord to meet you there, and lean into his presence. You'll come back a different person.

Thank you Jesus for your example of getting away to the mountains to be alone with our Father. Thank you for meeting us there and giving us strength. Amen

Week Six Journal

Restless Spirit: Lean in and release something to God.

_____

_____

_____

_____

_____

Beauty of Nature: Be still and listen-what is God saying to you.

_____

_____

_____

_____

_____

_____

Challenging Trails: Pressing in to your spiritual adventure.

_____

_____

_____

_____

_____

Pine Cones: Haw can we be more gracious with your words?

_____

_____

_____

_____

_____

Mountain Top Moments: Write about a mountain top moment.

_____

_____

_____

_____

_____

Other Reflections:

_____

_____

_____

_____

Meet My Jesus

He died for you. (Yes, you.)

Romans 10:9 NIV
If you declare with your mouth, "Jesus is Lord,"
and believe in your heart that God raised him
from the dead you will be saved.

Maybe you already know my Jesus, but I could not close this book without giving you the invitation to receive him into your heart, in case you've never taken that step.

Not sure? Then **let's make sure** you don't go another minute without knowing without a doubt that he knows you and loves you. That he actually died so that you could come into his household and become an adopted son or daughter of the Most High God. Come without hesitation into the life he has for you. A life full of freedom and peace deep in your soul, because you *know* you are accepted just the way you are. Believe, and receive the gift of the Holy Spirit placed in the middle of your heart to intimately know without a doubt *who's* you are.

The story of Jesus is well known; I'm sure you've heard it before. Father God sent his one and only son to be the ultimate sacrifice for us. He paid the price for sin in the world, so we don't have to. It was a horrible death, but then a miracle happened. He awoke from death and was the first to go to be with the Father. But his sacrifice made it possible for anyone who would believe to join him. Not just in heaven, but on a spiritual journey here and now, to grow into the best version of ourselves, and maybe bring a few folks along with us.

It's this easy: If you believe in your heart, tell him directly: "Jesus, I believe You died for me! I believe you were raised from the dead. I ask you to breath the gift of the Holy Spirit on me so I can know you deep in my soul." Now tell someone! Find your tribe of other believers and get connected to a local church. Congratulations on beginning your spiritual journey! Welcome to the Family!

Would you do one more thing? Would you contact me and tell me you met my Jesus? *www.CedarRidgeBooks.com/contact-us*

Photo credits:

Introduction:	Wallpaperflare.com
Healing Mountains:	†Eder Maioli
Royal Cedar:	Slichter 2005
The Mighty Oak:	Constitiution Oak of Alabama
Grassy Fields:	Heye Alexander von Humboldt
Earth Rhythms:	ted-ielts.com
Mountains Majesty:	Royalty Free Image
Eagleís Wings:	wallpapersafari.com
Secret Places:	wallpaperaccess.com
Surefooted Deer:	Stephen J. Krasemann
Mountain Storms:	Ales Krivec
Natures Wisdom:	Alexander Fattal
A Forest Home:	Ryan Stone
Mountain Birds:	hawkmountain.org
Mountain Songs:	wall.alphacoders.com
Hiding Places:	Kentucky Caving
Mountain Meadows:	Royalty Free
Deep Truths, Hidden Secrets:	Royalty Free
Giant Redwoods:	Aaron Logan
Walking in Love:	wallpapersafari.com
Mountain Refuge:	Canada sunset free for use
High on a Hill:	Jean Beaufort
Mountain Pass:	Alan Stark
Mysteries:	PickPik.com Royalty Free
Gold Mines:	Denver Public Library
Moving Mountains:	Robert Krimmel
Restless Spirits:	Samantha Weerasinghe
The Beauty of Nature:	publicdomainpictures.net
Challenging Trails:	mygrandcanyonpark.com
Pine Cones:	Freeimages.com
Mountaintop Moments:	gotmybackpack.com
Meet My Jesus:	Spring Meadows Family Worship

If you enjoyed this book,

please leave me a review on one or all of these online bookstores:

www.Amazon.com
www.BarnesAndNoble.com
www.BooksAMillion.com

THANK YOU!

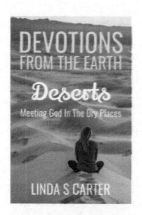

DEVOTIONS
From the Earth

Deserts

Inspiring devotions from nature
with a theme about meeting God
in the dry places.

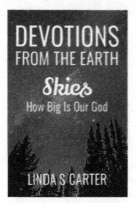

DEVOTIONS
From the Earth

Skies

Inspiring devotions from nature
with a theme about the
vast skies and God's Word.

DEVOTIONS
From the Earth

Waters

Inspiring devotions from nature
with a theme about the
healing waters on the Earth.

About the Author

Linda Carter is a wife and mother of one, a grandmother of six, and a lover of Jesus. She has been an entrepreneur for thirty three years as a work-from-home mom, while nurturing her gifts as an author and bible teacher along the way.

Her captivating teachings and writing spring from a life time of walking with God, and her connection with the natural world is enhanced from being a certified California Naturalist. She enjoys learning how to be a better steward of this amazing creation we have been given. Linda sees God's beautiful design in every created thing, with an eye to find the spiritual lessons contained in them.

With years of experience being involved with church ministry, mentoring and outreach, Linda has become a beacon of inspiration for those seeking spiritual growth and empowerment. She also loves teaching others how to appreciate and care for our beautiful planet. Her love for the natural world has played a pivotal role in shaping her unique views on life and spirituality. She shares her insights and wisdom from a fresh perspective, bringing nature's peace into her writings.

Whether she's found in the pages of her written works, mentoring others through the intricacies of scripture, or exploring the great outdoors, Linda Carter inspires us to step out in our faith, gain knowledge, and develop a deep appreciation for the beauty that surrounds us. She continues to inspire individuals on their spiritual journeys.

Made in United States
Orlando, FL
25 November 2024

54484770R00055